DINOSAUR PROFILES

CAUDIPTERYX

Titles in the Dinosaur Profiles series include:

Brachiosaurus

Caudipteryx

Deinonychus

Edmontosaurus

Scipionyx

Stegosaurus

Triceratops

Tyrannosaurus

DINOSAUR PROFILES

CAUDIPTERYX

Text by Fabio Marco Dalla Vecchia
Illustrations by Leonello Calvetti and Luca Massini

BLACKBIRCH®
PRESS

THOMSON
★
GALE

San Diego • Detroit • New York • San Francisco • Cleveland • New Haven, Conn. • Waterville, Maine • London • Munich

For more information, contact
The Gale Group, Inc.
27500 Drake Rd.
Farmington Hills, MI 48331-3535
Or you can visit our Internet site at http://www.gale.com

Computer illustrations 3D and 2D: Leonello Calvetti and Luca Massini

Photographs: pages 21, 22, 23 Yale Peabody Museum of Natural History, New Haven, CT

LIBRARY OF CONGRESS CATALOGING-IN-PUBLICATION DATA

Dalla Vecchia, Fabio Marco.
  Caudipteryx / text by Fabio Marco Dalla Vecchia; illustrations by Leonello Calvetti and Luca Massini.
    p. cm. — (Dinosaur profiles)
  Includes bibliographical references and index.
  ISBN 1-4103-0499-X (paperback : alk. paper)
  ISBN 1-4103-0333-0 (hardback : alk. paper)
  1. Caudipteryx—Juvenile literature. I. Calvetti, Leonello. II. Massini, Luca. III. Title. IV. Series: Dalla Vecchia, Fabio Marco. Dinosaur profiles.

  QE862.D335 2004
  567.912—dc22   2004008695

Printed in China
10 9 8 7 6 5 4 3 2 1

CONTENTS

A Changing World 6

An Odd Dinosaur 8

Caudipteryx Babies 10

First Steps 12

Danger! 14

At the Lakeside 16

The Caudipteryx Body 18

Digging Up Caudipteryx 20

Caudipteryx and Oviraptor 22

The Evolution of Dinosaurs 24

A Dinosaur's Family Tree 26

Glossary 28

For More Information 29

About the Author 30

Index 31

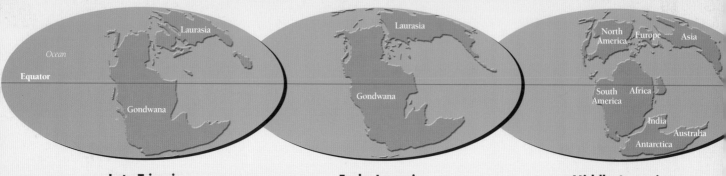

| Late Triassic | Early Jurassic | Middle Jurassic |
| 227–206 million years ago | 206–176 million years ago | 176–159 million years ago |

A Changing World

Earth's long history began 4.6 billion years ago. Dinosaurs are some of the most fascinating animals from the planet's long past.

The word *dinosaur* comes from the word *dinosauria*. This word was invented by the English scientist Richard Owen in 1842. It comes from two Greek words, *deinos* and *sauros*. Together, these words mean "terrifying lizards."

The dinosaur era, also called the Mesozoic era, lasted from 248 million years ago to 65 million years ago. It is divided into three periods. The first, the Triassic period, lasted 42 million years. The second, the Jurassic period, lasted 61 million years. The third, the Cretaceous period, lasted 79 million years. Dinosaurs ruled the world for a huge time span of 160 million years.

Like dinosaurs, mammals appeared at the end of the Triassic period. During the time of dinosaurs, mammals were small animals the size of a mouse. Only after dinosaurs became extinct did mammals develop

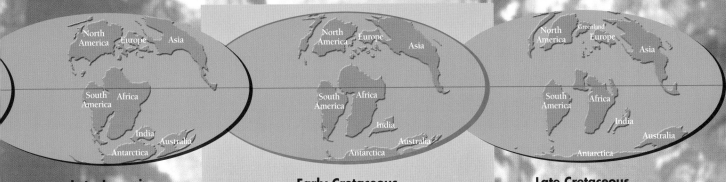

Late Jurassic
159–144 million years ago

Early Cretaceous
144–99 million years ago

Late Cretaceous
99–65 million years ago

into the many forms that exist today. Humans never met Mesozoic dinosaurs. The dinosaurs were gone nearly 65 million years before humans appeared on Earth.

Dinosaurs changed in time. *Stegosaurus* and *Brachiosaurus* no longer existed when *Tyrannosaurus* and *Triceratops* appeared 75 million years later.

The dinosaur world was different from today's world. The climate was warmer, with few extremes. The position of the continents was different. Plants were constantly changing, and grass did not even exist.

7

An Odd Dinosaur

Caudipteryx was a small and unusual dinosaur. It was a little larger than a big turkey and was covered with feathers. Its name comes from the Latin word for "tail" (*cauda*) and the Greek word for "wing" (*pteryx*). Some paleontologists believe that its feathers prove that birds are descendants of dinosaurs.

Caudipteryx's tail was extremely short compared to that of other dinosaurs that moved on two legs, but it had long feathers on the end that spread out like a fan. It also had long feathers, like the flight feathers of a bird, on its arms and forearms. Smaller feathers covered the rest of its body.

Although it had feathers, *Caudipteryx* could not fly. Its forearms were too short to act as wings. The feathers kept their bodies warm and protected them from the sun. Feathers also helped a nesting mother protect its eggs from cold winds or exposure to sunlight. Feathers on modern birds do the same things.

Caudipteryx's feathers were brightly colored. Scientists know this because traces of the feathers' color pattern were preserved in some fossilized feathers. The bright colors of *Caudipteryx*'s feathers might have helped it attract a partner during courtship. They might also have sent a warning message to other animals that invaded its territory.

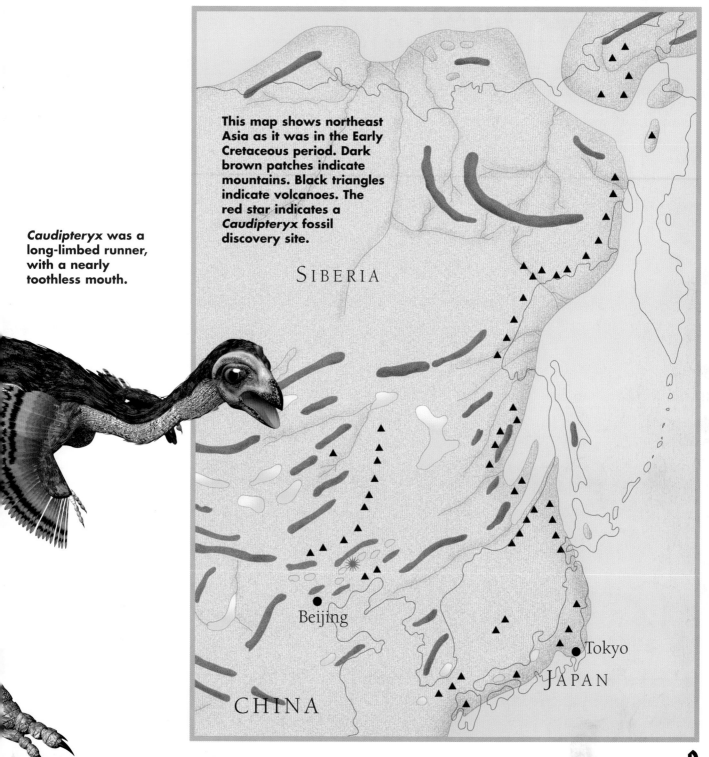

Caudipteryx was a long-limbed runner, with a nearly toothless mouth.

This map shows northeast Asia as it was in the Early Cretaceous period. Dark brown patches indicate mountains. Black triangles indicate volcanoes. The red star indicates a *Caudipteryx* fossil discovery site.

SIBERIA

Beijing

Tokyo

JAPAN

CHINA

9

Caudipteryx Babies

A *Caudipteryx* mother laid its long, oval eggs in a sheltered nest made with branches and ferns. The nest had to be hidden from predators. It also had to be protected from the volcanic ash that frequently fell to the ground. *Caudipteryx* sat on its nest to keep the eggs warm like birds do. The hatchlings probably looked like chicks. Their parents brought them tender leaves to eat.

First Steps

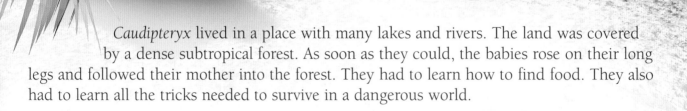

Caudipteryx lived in a place with many lakes and rivers. The land was covered by a dense subtropical forest. As soon as they could, the babies rose on their long legs and followed their mother into the forest. They had to learn how to find food. They also had to learn all the tricks needed to survive in a dangerous world.

The region was full of life. There were many kinds of insects, fish, frogs, lizards, and turtles. There were also small mammals, pterosaurs, birds, and dinosaurs. Some were dangerous.

Danger!

Several predator dinosaurs about the same size as *Caudipteryx* lived in the same area. The most dangerous was *Sinornithosaurus*. It had large, jagged teeth and a sharp claw on each foot. Luckily for *Caudipteryx*, the *Sinornithosaurus* was rare. *Sinosauropteryx* was more common. This predator was less than 5 feet (1.5 m) long. It fed mainly on lizards and other small animals, but it would also attack the young *Caudipteryx*. If that happened, the mother *Caudipteryx* would spread out the fan of feathers at the end of its tail and stretch out its feathered arms to look bigger and scare off the attacker.

At the Lakeside

Caudipteryx was a gentle vegetarian that ate plants in the forests near lakes. It pulled up plants, seedlings, or roots using its front teeth and swallowed them without chewing.

Often the lava flows from nearby volcanoes burned and covered the places in which *Caudipteryx* lived. When this happened, the survivors had to move to other parts of the forest not reached by the lava to search for food.

THE CAUDIPTERYX BODY

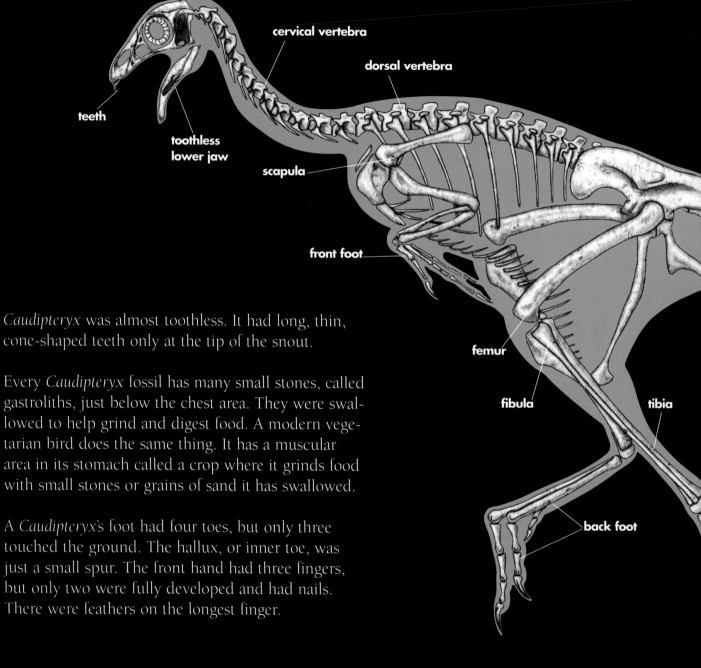

cervical vertebra

dorsal vertebra

teeth

toothless
lower jaw

scapula

front foot

femur

fibula

tibia

back foot

Caudipteryx was almost toothless. It had long, thin, cone-shaped teeth only at the tip of the snout.

Every *Caudipteryx* fossil has many small stones, called gastroliths, just below the chest area. They were swallowed to help grind and digest food. A modern vegetarian bird does the same thing. It has a muscular area in its stomach called a crop where it grinds food with small stones or grains of sand it has swallowed.

A *Caudipteryx*'s foot had four toes, but only three touched the ground. The hallux, or inner toe, was just a small spur. The front hand had three fingers, but only two were fully developed and had nails. There were feathers on the longest finger.

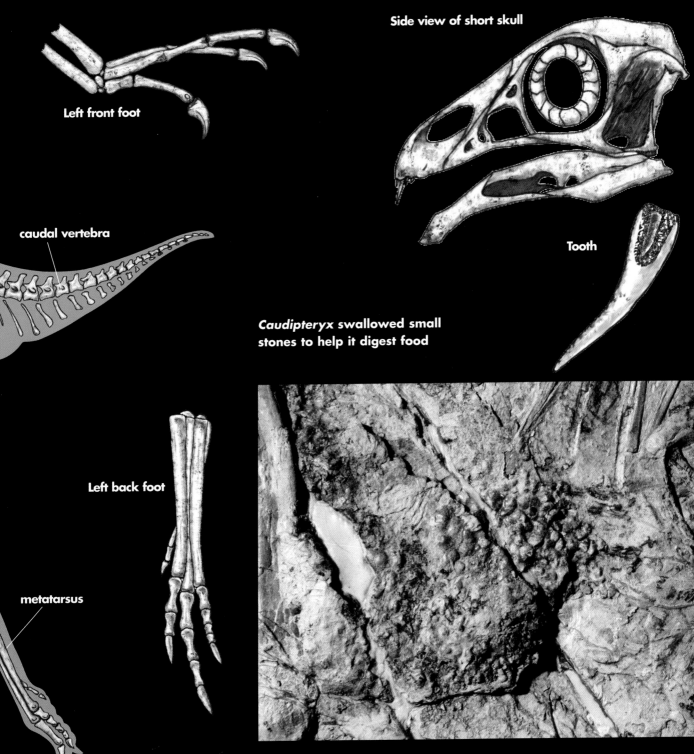

Left front foot

Side view of short skull

caudal vertebra

Tooth

Caudipteryx swallowed small stones to help it digest food

Left back foot

metatarsus

DIGGING UP CAUDIPTERYX

Caudipteryx lived in the Liaoning Province of China in the Early Cretaceous period, about 125 million years ago. Other dinosaurs with feathers have also been found in Liaoning.

Some paleontologists believe *Caudipteryx* is closely related to birds because of its feathers. Others think that *Caudipteryx* was not an ancestor of birds. Instead, they think it belongs to the strange dinosaur group called oviraptorosauria. These dinosaurs are known for their short snouts and lack of teeth.

At least four nearly complete skeletons of *Caudipteryx* have been found. The first *Caudipteryx* skeleton was probably found near the town of Sihetun, Liaoning Province, China, between 1995 and 1997. It is not known who found it. The remains of several dinosaurs and birds have been found by local farmers.

The first fossil of *Caudipteryx* is a nearly complete skeleton. It has traces of feathers at the end of the tail and along the arms. It is in a rock slab with many

Left: This *Caudipteryx* fossil was found in Liaoning Province, China.

Below: *Caudipteryx* was a feathered dinosaur.

shells of small marine animals. The dead body probably sank to the bottom of a lake where the shells of tiny crustaceans also piled up. Fine sediment covered it quickly. This protected it from predators and scavengers. In addition, the ash from volcanic eruptions often settled in the lakes of Liaoning, along with mud carried by rivers. All of this helped cover the body of *Caudipteryx* and preserve it.

Caudipteryx skeletons are officially exhibited at the National Geological Museum of China, the Institute of Vertebrate Paleontology and Paleoanthropology of Beijing, and at the Paleontological Museum of Liaoning. However, most of the time the skeletons are on tour. They are displayed in exhibits in many other countries around the world. These exhibits attract large crowds of curious visitors who want to see the feathered dinosaurs of China.

Many scientists believe that the Chicxulub crater off the coast of Mexico was made by a meteorite that led to the extinction of the dinosaurs.

Places where Oviraptorosaurian fossils have been found are noted on the map.

CAUDIPTERYX AND OVIRAPTOR

• *Oviraptor, Mongolia, 80–70 million years ago*

Oviraptor, *Citipati*, and *Khaan* from Mongolia are oviraptorosaurids and close relatives of *Caudipteryx*. *Caenagnathus* from Canada is more distantly related. Recently, some paleontologists have suggested that oviraptorosaurians might not be dinosaurs. Instead, they might be odd birds that lost the ability to fly. Most scientists believe they are dinosaurs, however. *Caudipteryx* remains a mysterious and interesting animal.

- **Caudipteryx, China, 125 million years ago**

THE GREAT EXTINCTION

Sixty-five million years ago, 60 million years after the time of *Caudipteryx*, dinosaurs became extinct. This may have happened because a large meteorite struck Earth. A wide crater caused by a meteorite exactly 65 million years ago has been located along the coast of the Yucatán Peninsula in Mexico. The impact of the meteorite would have produced an enormous amount of dust. This dust would have stayed suspended in the atmosphere and blocked sunlight for a long time. A lack of sunlight would have caused a drastic drop of the earth's temperature and killed plants. The plant-eating dinosaurs would have died, starved and frozen. As a result, meat-eating dinosaurs would have had no prey and would also have starved.

Some scientists believe dinosaurs did not die out completely. They think that birds were feathered dinosaurs that survived the great extinction. That would make the present-day chicken and all of its feathered relatives descendants of the large dinosaurs.

THE EVOLUTION OF DINOSAURS

The oldest dinosaur fossils are 220–225 million years old and have been found mainly in South America. They have also been found in Africa, India, and North America. Dinosaurs probably evolved from small and nimble bipedal reptiles like the Triassic *Lagosuchus* of Argentina. Dinosaurs were able to rule the world because their legs were held directly under the body, like those of modern mammals. This made them faster and less clumsy than other reptiles.

Since 1887, dinosaurs have been divided into two groups based on the structure of their hips. Saurischian dinosaurs had hips shaped like those of modern lizards. Ornithischian dinosaurs had hips shaped like those of modern birds.

Triceratops is one of the Ornithischian dinosaurs, whose hip bones (inset) are shaped like those of modern birds.

24

Tyrannosaurus is in the Saurischian group of dinosaurs, whose hip bones (inset) are shaped like those of modern lizards.

There are two main groups of saurischians. One group is sauropodomorphs. This group includes sauropods, such as *Brachiosaurus*. Sauropods ate plants and were quadrupedal, meaning they walked on four legs. The other group of saurischians, theropods, includes bipedal meat-eating predators. Some paleontologists believe birds are a branch of theropod dinosaurs.

Ornithischians are all plant eaters. They are divided into three groups. Thyreophorans include the quadrupedal stegosaurians, including *Stegosaurus*, and ankylosaurians, including *Ankylosaurus*. The other two groups are ornithopods, which includes *Edmontosaurus* and marginocephalians.

A Dinosaur's Family Tree

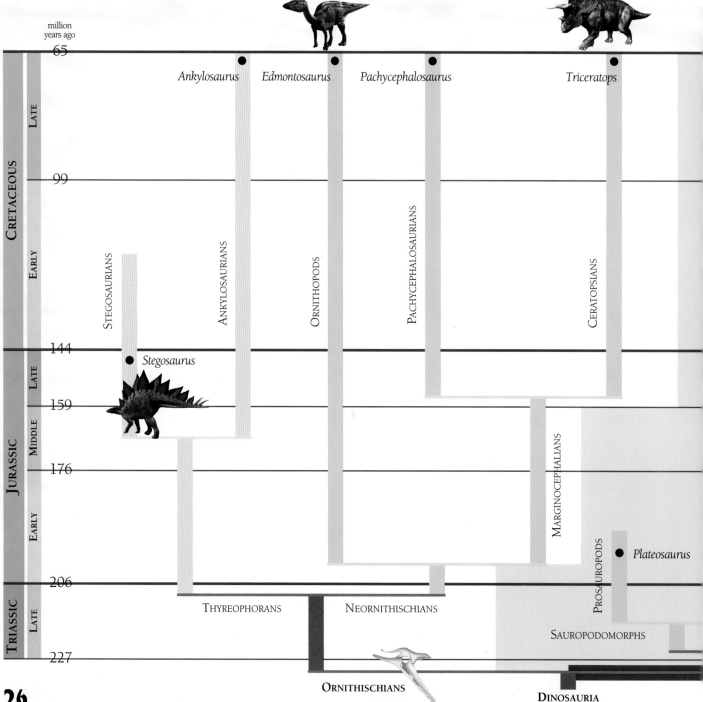

million
years ago

CRETACEOUS

JURASSIC

TRIASSIC

LATE

EARLY

LATE

MIDDLE

EARLY

LATE

65

99

144

159

176

206

227

Ankylosaurus   Edmontosaurus   Pachycephalosaurus   Triceratops

STEGOSAURIANS

ANKYLOSAURIANS

ORNITHOPODS

PACHYCEPHALOSAURIANS

CERATOPSIANS

MARGINOCEPHALIANS

PROSAUROPODS

• Stegosaurus

• Plateosaurus

THYREOPHORANS   NEORNITHISCHIANS

SAUROPODOMORPHS

ORNITHISCHIANS

DINOSAURIA

SAUROPODS

Brachiosaurus

SAURISCHIANS

THEROPODS

ORNITHOLESTES

Scipionyx

ORNITHOMMOIDEANS

Ornithomimus

TYRANNOSAUROIDS

Tyrannosaurus

OVIRAPTOROSAURIANS

Caudipteryx

DEINONYCHOSAURIANS

Deinonychus

BIRDS

GLOSSARY

Bipedal moving on two feet

Bone hard tissue made mainly of calcium phosphate

Caudal related to the tail

Cenozoic Era the period of geological time between 65 million years ago and the present day

Cervical related to the neck

Cretaceous Period the period of geological time between 144 and 65 million years ago

Dorsal related to the back

Egg a large cell enclosed in a shell produced by reptiles and birds to reproduce themselves

Feathers outgrowth of the skin of birds and some dinosaurs, used in flight and in providing insulation and protection of the body

Femur thigh bone

Fibula the outer of the two bones in the lower leg

Fossil a part of an organism of an earlier geologic age, such as a skeleton or leaf imprint, that has been preserved in the earth's crust

Jurassic Period the period of geological time between 206 and 144 million years ago

Mesozoic Era the period of geological time between 248 and 65 million years ago

Meteorite a piece of iron or rock that falls to Earth from space

Paleontologist scientist who studies prehistoric life

Quadrupedal moving on four feet

Scapula shoulder blade

Scavenger animal that eats dead animals or plants

Skeleton the structure of an animal body, made up of bones

Skull the bones that form the cranium and the face

Tibia the shinbone

Triassic Period the period of geological time between 248 and 206 million years ago

Vertebrae the bones of the backbone

Volcano conelike geological structure made by the buildup of lava

For More Information

Books

Paul M. Barrett, *National Geographic Dinosaurs*.
Washington, DC: National Geographic Society, 2001.

Tim Haines, *Walking with Dinosaurs: A Natural History*.
New York: Dorling Kindersley, 2000.

David Lambert, Darren Naish, and Elizabeth Wyse,
*Dinosaur Encyclopedia: From Dinosaurs to the Dawn of
Man*. New York: Dorling Kindersley, 2001.

Web Sites

The Cyberspace Museum of Natural History
www.cyberspacemuseum.com/dinohall.html
An online dinosaur museum that includes descriptions and illustrations.

Dinodata
www.dinodata.net
A site that includes detailed descriptions of fossils,
illustrations, and news about dinosaur research and
recent discoveries.

**The Smithsonian National Museum of Natural
History**
www.nmnh.si.edu/paleo/dino
A virtual tour of the Smithsonian's National Museum
of Natural History dinosaur exhibits.

ABOUT THE AUTHOR

Fabio Marco Dalla Vecchia is the curator of the
Paleontological Museum of Monfalcone in Gorizia,
Italy. He has participated in several paleontological
field works in Italy and other countries and has
directed paleontological excavations in Italy. He is the
author of more than fifty scientific articles that have
been published in national and international journals.

INDEX

arms, 8, 14, 20

babies, 10, 12
birds, 8, 20, 23, 24, 25
body, 20–21

Caudipteryx
  body, 18–19
  description, 8
  relatives, 23
China, 20–21
claws, 14
Cretaceous period, 6–7, 9, 21

danger, 14
digestion, 18, 19
dinosaurs, 6–7, 14
  family tree, 26–27

eggs, 8, 10

evolution, 24
extinction, 6, 22, 23

family tree, 26–27
feathers, 8, 14, 18, 20
feet, 14, 18
fingers, 18
food, 12, 16, 18
fossils, 9, 18, 20–21, 22, 24

gastroliths, 18

hand, 18
hips, 24–25
humans, 7

Jurassic period, 6–7

lakes, 12, 16
legs, 12, 24

Index

lizards, 24

mammals, 6
meat eaters, 24
Mesozoic era, 6
meteorite, 22, 23
mouth, 9

nest, 10

ornithischian, 24–25, 26
oviraptorosauria, 20, 22, 23

plant eater, 16, 25
predators, 10, 14, 24

reptiles, 24

saurischian, 24–25, 27
sauropodomorphs, 25
sediment, 21
skeleton, 20–21
snout, 18, 20
stomach, 18

tail, 8, 14, 20
teeth, 14, 18, 20
theropods, 25
toes, 18
Triassic period, 6

vegetarian, 16
volcanoes, 10, 16, 21